THE LAW OF THE LAND

When considering a sale, it is vitally important to be aware of the legal implications involved and, if going to a sale yard, to read and follow the conditions as laid down – usually found in the sale catalogue.

In the United Kingdom, The Sale of Goods Act, 1979 (amended 1994), is the most important legal instrument relating to the sale of horses. This act requires that a horse, like any other item, must be fit for the purpose for which it is being sold.

In other words, a jumper must be able to jump, a potential racehorse must be able to race, an animal sold as a stallion must be able to cover mares, etc., and there must be no undefined defect that will limit the animal's use for its stated purpose and for a normal lifespan carrying out the stated purpose.

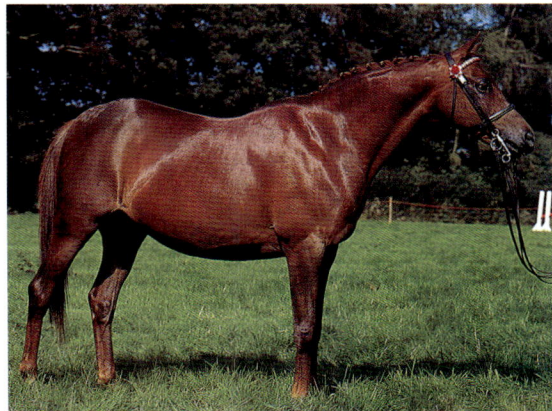

Under the 1994 amendments, the animal must now be of 'satisfactory' quality, much the same as any other item of goods; the word 'satisfactory' to be judged relative to what might constitute that value in the opinion of a reasonable person. This includes matters such as temperament and vice, though the requirement does not apply to defects brought to the buyer's attention before sale. For example, a bad-tempered young horse might stand out at a sale, but an experienced horseman, made aware of this, might feel able to handle the animal. It would not be returnable on the basis of temperament in this case.

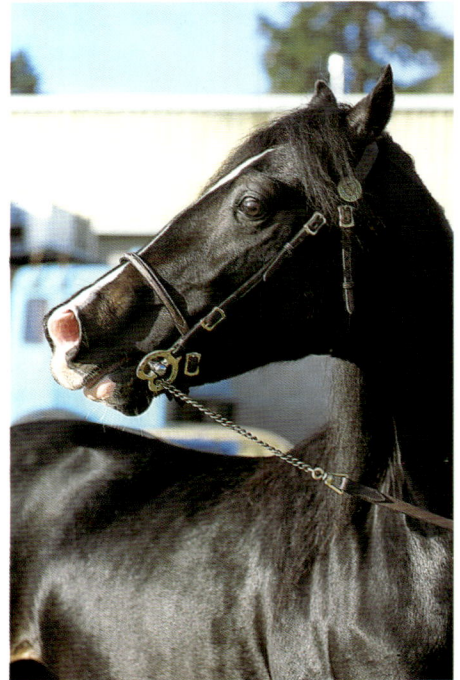

IMPORTANT POINTS

- A vendor has a duty to declare any material fact, of which he/she is aware, that may influence the future usefulness of an animal.
- A buyer has a duty to be informed and observant.

The buyer, on the other hand, is expected to inspect a prospective purchase to detect any obvious defects. If an individual feels inadequate, there is an unspoken obligation to get expert advice. This may come from a vet but could come from an agent, or an experienced person of any kind who understands the horse, its conformation, and knows the surface problems that are likely to exist. If, for example, an animal for sale has a splint, or a growth, or is deformed in any evident way, a buyer is expected to notice that fact, within reason.

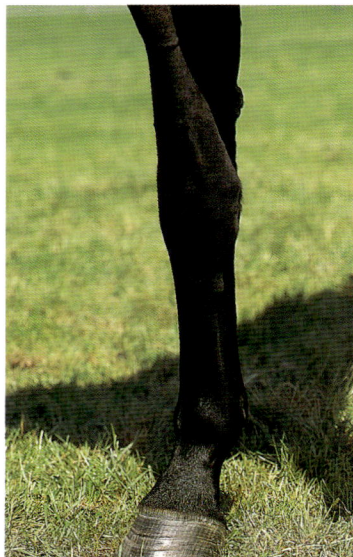
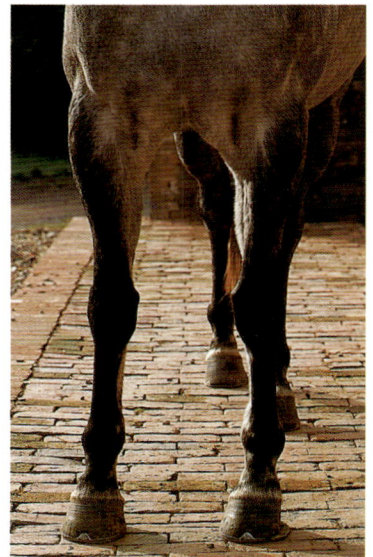

A plea of ignorance for, say, something as obvious as a badly injured tendon, would not be likely to be accepted, except, perhaps, where access to the horse was not allowed. However, a more obscure old, healed tendon injury might be different if the injury were only detectable by an experienced eye (as illustrated here in the photos on the *right*), or a fresh injury from which the heat had been removed.

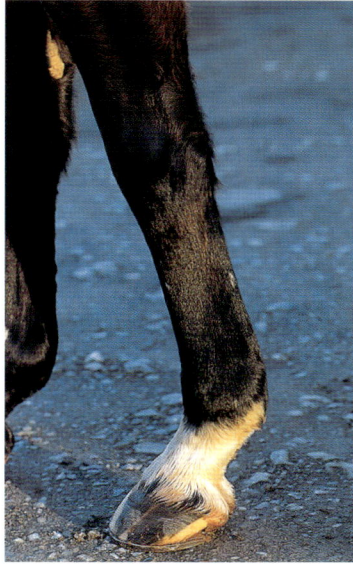

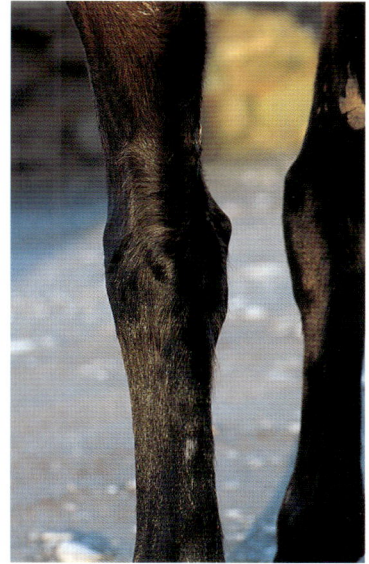

PRACTICAL NOTE

In private sales, the rule *caveat emptor* is a common law maxim warning a buyer not to claim purchases were defective unless protected by express guarantees from the vendor in advance. A private sale is also likely to be covered by the Sale of Goods Act, especially where there is any suggestion of dishonesty.

The law is concerned with honesty and protecting the interests of even the inexperienced buyer and will not tolerate any suggestion of deception.

In fulfilling the obligation to be informed, buyers are best advised to have animals examined by a veterinary surgeon before a sale is concluded. And this, when completed without hitch, is an added safeguard for the vendor, except where any material fact is deliberately concealed.

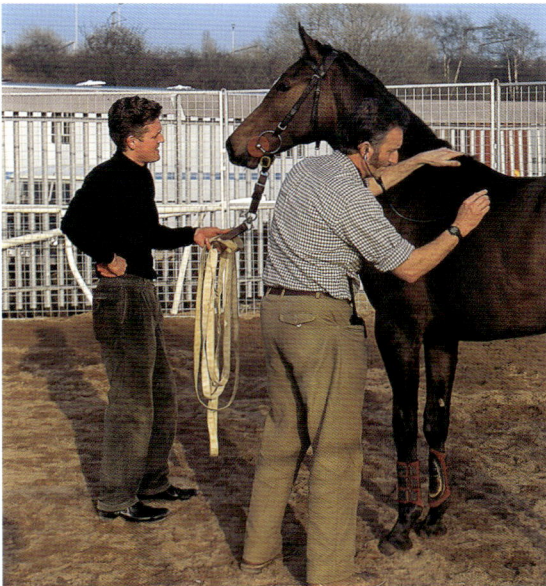

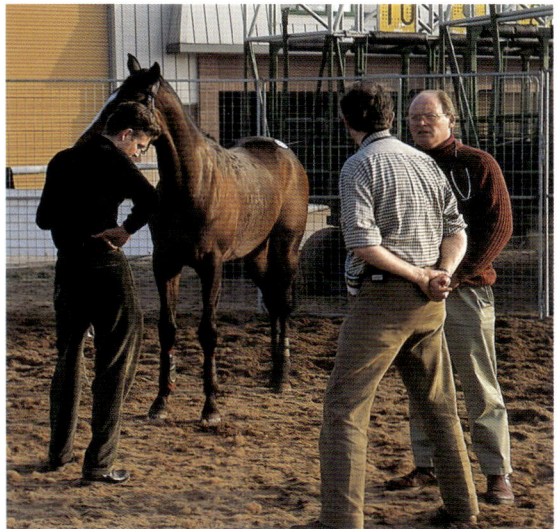

VETTING AT SALES

- Examination is usually arranged within the sales complex.
- Vets will be at hand, facilities provided, and a horse may have to be vetted within one or two hours of the hammer falling.
- Alternatively, buyers may be given a specified time (one or two days, perhaps) to take an animal away to be vetted. Rejected animals must be returned within the specified time and more than one opinion may be required. It is vital to read conditions and know exactly what applies in particular circumstances.

In a private sale, veterinary examination is routinely carried out once a horse has been seen and inspected and an agreement to purchase has been made. Completion is dependent on what the vet has to say.

The vet is not infallible and there are conditions which may not be detected on a standard examination (e.g. a tendency to bleed from the lungs, common in racehorses, that may not show even under extensive testing).

INFORMATION THE VET PROVIDES

- The vet will decide if an animal fits its description and if it is suitable for the purpose for which it is being bought.
- The buyer is receiving an expert opinion on the significance of any lesion found.
- The vet will state whether or not an animal is free of detectable defects that might limit future usefulness.
- The vet is not providing a warranty or guarantee.
- The vet's opinion is an express opinion of the animal at the time.

Where a vendor does not come clean about any relevant information of this nature, a horse might well be returned. If there had been surgery, for example, this should be declared, especially if any critical procedure had been undertaken. Similarly, if a horse has a known defect (like a heart murmur), whether or not it affects performance, this should be stated, rather than have it found under examination when it might have a harmful effect on a sale.

Horses should not be sold with inter-current disease or infections. Horses with open infections must not be presented at a public sale, particularly if the condition is contagious or where there are evident discharges. No animal should ever be presented in a condition like the mare in this picture.

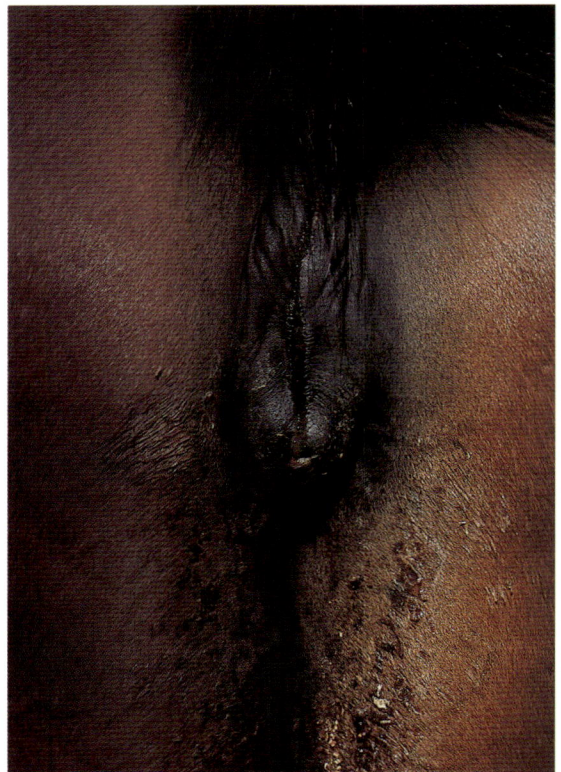

Although they are not directly transmissible, a vendor may be asked to declare the presence of sarcoids (skin tumours that come in various shapes and sizes), even though these are usually self-evident. Failure to do so may result in the horse being returned.

GOING TO A PUBLIC SALE

It is wise to have a horse properly presented for sale. The grey horse is in good physical condition, the bay mare is not. It is also critical to have good and effective tack and to have an animal ready for any procedure to which it may be subjected, including vetting, remembering it may be pulled out and trotted up many times a day.

A horse that is going to be lunged should be ready to lunge on request, and be willing to canter strongly on the lunge without stopping. A horse that is to be ridden must be suitably equipped.

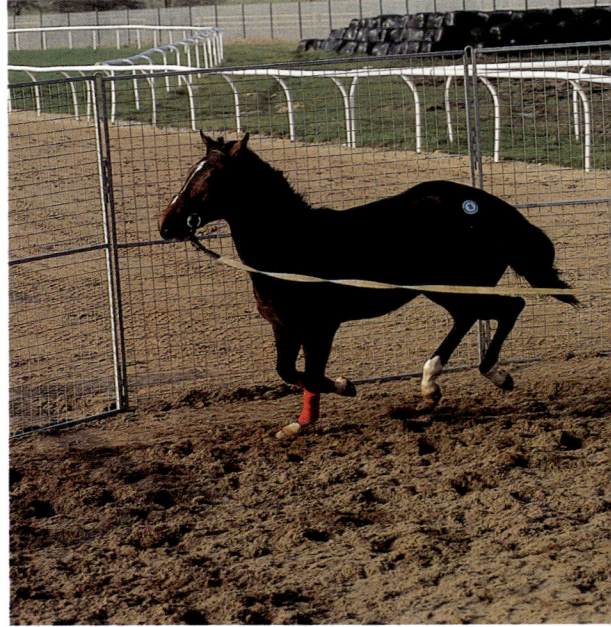

IMPORTANT POINTS

- Do not present a horse in poor condition.
- Make sure your horse is used to being handled.
- Prepare properly for sale, this includes feeding, grooming, shoeing and training.
- Have the correct tack to allow full control in the hustle and bustle of a sale yard.
- Horses to be lunged will need a cavesson, lunge rein and whip.
- Horses to be ridden will need a saddle and bridle.

VETTING FACILITIES AT SALES

It is the sales company's duty to provide adequate and safe facilities for vetting horses (where vetting is standard) and, where this is not the case, a vendor might be justified in refusing to allow any risk to an animal being sold. The same applies to any arrangement for riding. Of course, this may result in the loss of a sale but at least there is still a horse to be sold.

LIABILITY IN CASE OF INJURY

Liability for injury to an animal occurring during the process of a sale might be: the vendor's, at a time when the sale has not been completed; the buyer's, if it occurs after a sale is considered to have been completed; or the sales company's, depending on the exact circumstances of the occurrence.

In a private sale, liability becomes the buyer's once the sale has been completed.

SPECIAL CONDITIONS

Thoroughbred yearlings have a special requirement regarding wind examination (also applies to 'breeze-up' sales, or to any horse sold as 'in-training'), which may vary with the specific sale, conditions pertaining to which are best gleaned from appropriate sales catalogues. (Breeze-up sales are when two-year-olds are ridden up a race course in the morning for buyers to view them prior to the sale in the evening.) It is likely an animal will have to be lunged and may have to be subjected to examination with an endoscope. Alternatively, a certificate to ensure freedom from diseases of the larynx may be required before an animal is presented for sale, as may other special

requirements, like radiographs of joints and feet (though there is a tendency for these to be carried out to satisfy purchasers rather than as any special condition of sale).

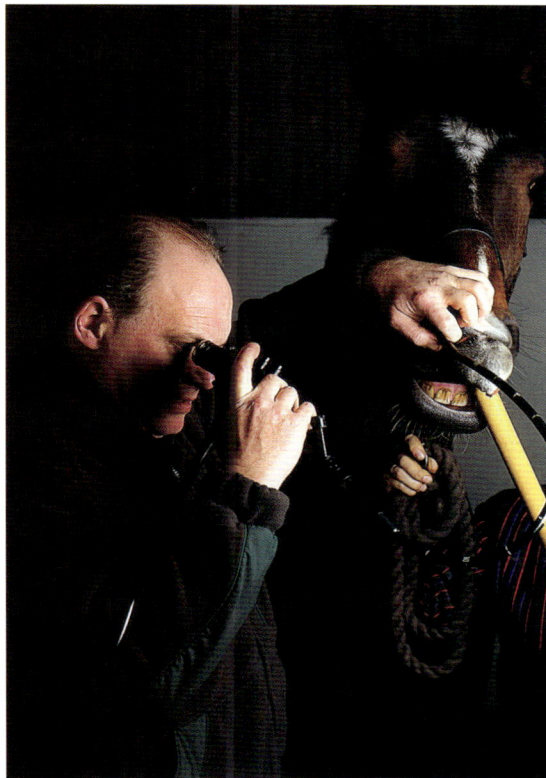

DESCRIPTION

Vendors are responsible for the description of their animals, be that in a catalogue or anywhere else it might appear. It may be that a sales company will help to set out what will appear in print, finding details of pedigree, performance, etc. but the ultimate duty of truth lies with the vendor. Any material error may well cause an animal to be returned.

Description covers such matters as colour, breed, sex, age and height, as well as the animal's intended use, defects and warranties.

Inevitably, there is a certain acceptable latitude in some of these demands. A horse stated to be dark bay would be unlikely to be rejected if it turned out to be brown, nor would any colour variation provide such an excuse; except, perhaps, where a buyer wanted a specific colour, say for a driving team, and this was not received, there having been no chance to see the horse first.

Breed is certainly important where this is stated to be of a specific type. A Thoroughbred that wasn't registered, or for which there was no documentation, might lose value if barred from racing, for example, where this was the intended use. It is, therefore, important to be able to verify pedigree details of any pure-bred or registered animal, otherwise a sale might be compromised.

The sex of an animal is important, though unlikely to be wrongly declared. However, a horse that is a rig is returnable, unless declared; a 'maiden filly' would have to be a maiden and might be returnable if found to be otherwise; and a mare declared to be in foal might need to have current certified evidence to support the claim, especially where this is not immediately evident.

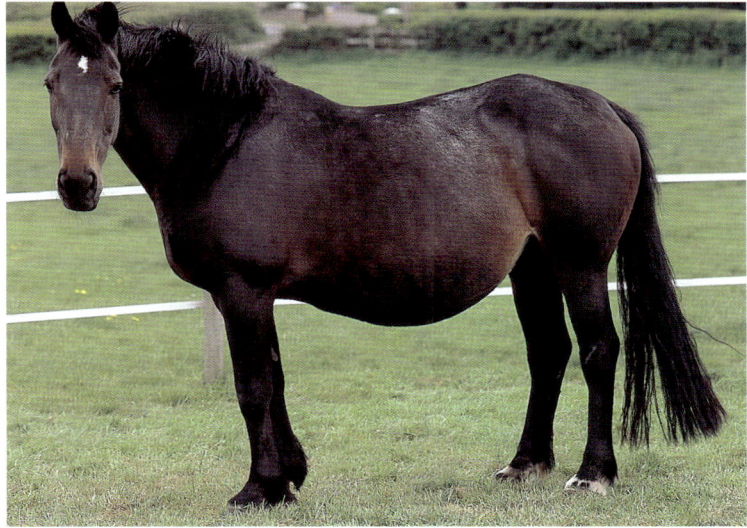

Age can be a contentious subject, especially where there is no documented evidence available to support a vendor's word. In such a situation, an animal is traditionally aged by its teeth. However, it has to be understood that this is a far from perfect procedure and it is not uncommon for horses to have teeth that do not conform with that expected for their purported age.

Height is also a matter over which there can be disputes, although the claim should not be frivolous. Specific height is only generally required with ponies, where there may be a certificate of height available under the Joint Measurement Scheme; this should be current, in which case it is binding. A horse declared to be of a given height at a sale should be approximately that height, otherwise it could be returnable. However, the buyer has a certain responsibility to ensure this is correct before bidding.

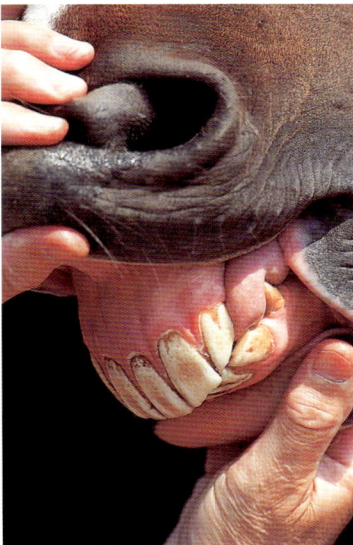

In describing a horse's intended use, it is best to be realistic and there is no point in saying a horse is suitable to work in harness, for example, if it has not been introduced to harness. A young horse should not be stated to be likely to make an eventer or showjumper unless there were strong grounds to support the prospect. A dressage horse might well have to show off its gaits.

An animal that has a defect that excludes it from use for a particular purpose should not be sold for that purpose, e.g. a horse with a tendon injury sold as being suitable for racing. It would be different if the lesion were declared: a buyer might decide the leg could be improved, or might stand up to training, in which case a risk is being taken dependent on full disclosure of the condition. A judgment is also being made based on experience and, perhaps, expert advice. The horse might eventually end up racing, as did the horse with this thickened leg (*see right*). Although injured tendons can be improved with rest and treatment, it is wrong to attempt to sell a horse with a recent tendon injury without declaring that fact. The leg might look clean but, if subjected to vigorous exercise, there is a strong chance the animal would break down and a prospective buyer has the right to be forewarned. If the injury is not declared, it is very probable that the horse could be returned.

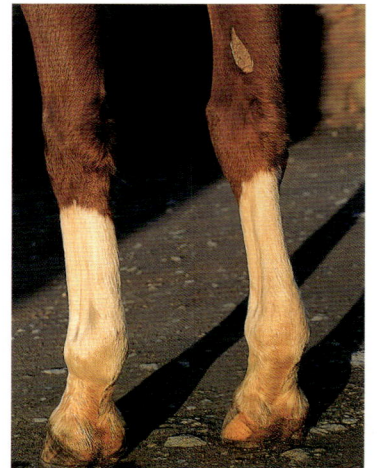

VICES

A vice is defined as 'a defect in the temper of a horse which makes it dangerous or diminishes its usefulness, or a bad habit which is injurious to its health' (Scholefield v. Robb [1839]). A seller is liable to declare the presence of any vice. This includes all conditions like wind-sucking, crib-biting, etc., as well as matters of temperament that might make an animal unsuitable (or dangerous) for riding.

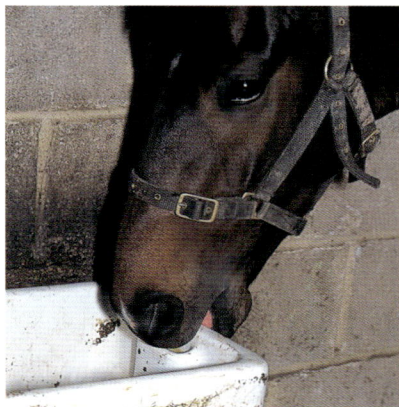

VICE DEFINITIONS

- A **weaver** is a horse that habitually swings its head and neck and transfers weight from one forefoot to the other while in a standing position.
- A **boxwalker** is a horse that walks about its box aimlessly and continually.
- A **wind-sucker** is a horse that continually swallows air, irrespective of whether this is associated with grasping fixed objects with its incisor teeth or not.
- A **crib-biter** is a horse that habitually grasps objects, most often wood, with its incisor teeth.
- A **shiverer** is a horse that shows spasmodic movements of the tail and hind limbs associated with disease of the central nervous system.

The presence of an anti-weaving device on a stable door (like these here) might create suspicion, and weavers will often exhibit the vice in strange surroundings. Boxwalking is a nervous condition, often marked by the presence of a track around the bed in the stable. It is sometimes resolved by providing a companion.

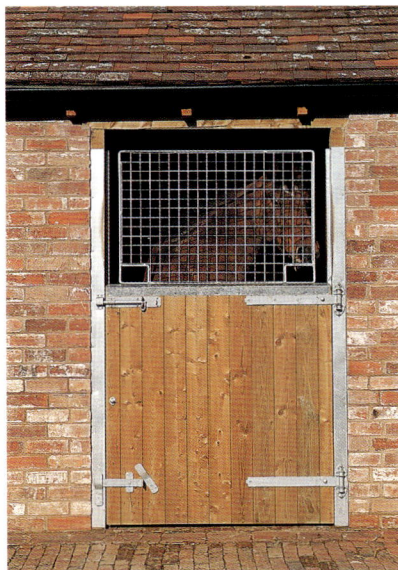

A horse that rears when ridden, is otherwise intractable, or that is violent and dangerous, is considered to have a vice of temperament. Such an animal is returnable in law unless the problem is declared prior to sale. It might be deemed not to be safe, or to be unsuitable for the purpose for which it is being sold.

It should be understood that vice is a matter between the seller and buyer. The veterinary surgeon will mention any vice that becomes apparent during the course of examination but will not be liable for any that exists but is not expressed, or declared. A buyer or, perhaps, the vet, may ask a vendor to sign a declaration that an animal is free of vice and this would have to be complied with.

PRESENTING A LIMITED CERTIFICATE

A vendor with a horse that has a declarable defect has the option to have that defect examined prior to sale by a veterinary surgeon and to obtain a certificate, relating to the defect only, which can be presented when a sale is proposed. If, for example, there is a prominent scar (like that shown here), or bony swelling, say on the pastern, or a visibly abnormal foot, it would be possible to have this examined. The vet might decide to take radiographs which could be made available for examination by the buyer, or by the buyer's vet. By acting in this way, the vendor is protecting the value of the animal and it becomes easier for a buyer to reach a decision relative to the specific lesion.

The eye is another area in which the provision of a certificate might help a sale, as long as the opinion is authoritative, specific and not damning and helps to lift the cloud from an otherwise contentious matter. For example, the horse whose eye condition is featured here suffered a thorn injury. The affected eye is almost totally blind but the animal hunts, jumps and competes across country without hindrance.

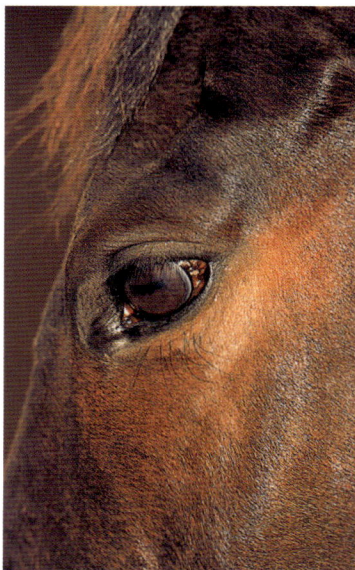

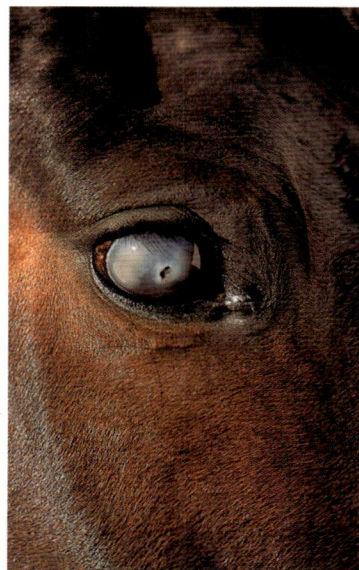

An abnormal looking joint (like the offside fetlock here), might benefit from the presentation of radiographs, or a buyer might be given the option to have this done at their own expense. However, 'for the sake of a hap'orth of tar', do not spoil your chances, it is wise to anticipate problems and be armed. Remember, an examining vet might condemn the horse and this might be accepted by a buyer, without recourse to further tests, and your sale might be finished.

IMPORTANT POINTS

- Take care in presenting limited certificates.
- Complexly worded certificates may only confuse buyers.
- It is notoriously difficult to interpret the significance of heart problems.
- A specialist opinion can be useful.
- Special tests can be of help – ask your vet.
- If a horse has form in competition, declare: 'Has competed successfully despite big knee', or 'Has mild heart murmur which has not affected performance', etc.
- Always be open in trying to protect your interests.

OTHER EXISTING CONDITIONS

Horses are sometimes sold with conditions of the back and musculature that are chronic in nature, like the case shown here, where there is considerable wasting on the near side of the pelvis as seen from behind. Symptoms may diminish with rest but are sometimes re-aggravated every time an animal is returned to work. It may be that the condition can be treated successfully (though it may not) but it is the vendor's responsibility to do this. The alternative is to risk having the animal fail a veterinary examination, which would be justified. Conditions of this nature are extremely common, even if not always correctly diagnosed. Today, many animals with these problems are being returned because they fail to remain sound.

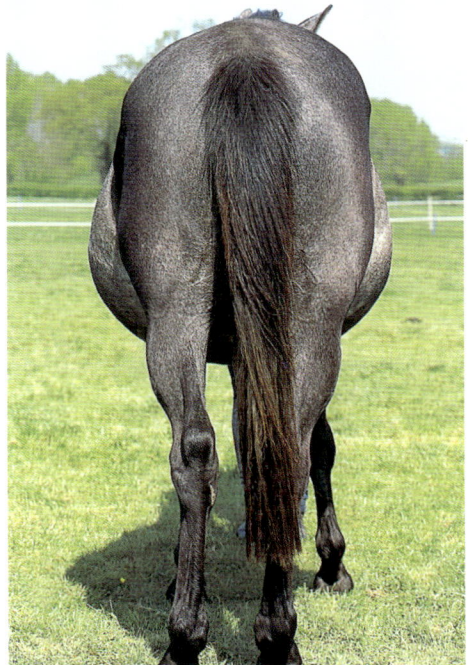

VENDOR'S GENERAL CERTIFICATES

Providing a general veterinary certificate prior to sale, which is carried out on the vendor's behalf, is normally only done in given sales, with given types of horse, and the animals are generally subject to further examination before passing into the hands of a buyer. This is usual for store horses (horses kept until three or four years of age before starting an active career) being sold for National Hunt racing. In all other situations, a buyer is advised not to accept a certificate issued for a vendor, or by a vendor's vet, and it is well to know that. A vendor's vet may have privileged information which they cannot divulge.

CONDITIONS FOR WHICH A HORSE MAY BE RETURNED

Horses may be returned for a number of reasons, most of which are for conditions which should have been declared in advance, or in respect of improper description. In fact, a horse will be returnable for any condition likely to affect future usefulness or limit the time span for which it can be used.

Should a horse become lame, for no evident reason, even within days or weeks of a sale, it is not unknown for proceedings to be taken and for the outcome of the matter to be decided in a court.

A HORSE MAY BE RETURNED IF:

• undeclared vices are detected after sale;

• it is found to have been tubed or otherwise operated on for its wind (evidence for which will be found in the region of the larynx, the area shown here, *see right*);

• it has had any major surgical procedure of current significance, e.g. neurectomy, bowel anastomosis, etc;

• it is found to be a rig;

• it is disqualified, or unqualified, for events for which it had been declared qualified;

• it has lost its right to be registered, say as a Thoroughbred.

A horse may also be returned for any unspecified problem which has not been declared.

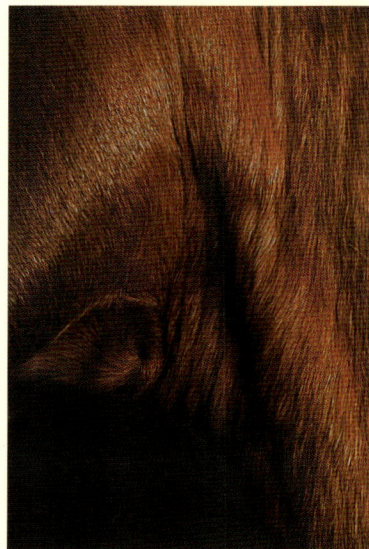

WARRANTIES

Where you are selling a horse that has a fault which is insignificant, it may be wise to offer a warranty that covers the particular problem, failing which the animal could be returned. For example, a deformed horse might compete with effect, and the ability to perform could be warranted, despite the defect.

By stating that a horse is a 'good jumper', a warranty is being given as to the horse's abilities and the animal would be returnable if this turned out not to be so.

Horses often change hands where a limited warranty is given. A common example is where a full wind examination is not carried out, perhaps due to lack of facilities. A vendor, happy the animal was sound of wind, might allow a warranty declaring the animal could be returned within a given period, say a week, if any problem is found with its wind. This would give the buyer time in which to have a wind examination carried out.

Where a horse goes unexpectedly lame and cannot be vetted, the procedure could be suspended until the vendor was able to say the problem had been corrected. This might also happen if the horse was found to be lame during the course of examination, had not previously been lame, and a good reason for the problem existed, like a loose shoe, or a foot infection.

It is also important that any declared standard of training is met. A horse that is 'untried' should not have been tried. A horse described as 'advanced' should not be a novice, or one brought to a 'breeze-up' sale, like those shown here, only just backed.

PREPARATION FOR SALE

To prepare any horse for sale requires firstly having the animal in good physical condition, and exercised, as is this chestnut. Horses up from grass, that have only just been shod, may be sore footed and go lame when lunged or ridden. They may also fail an exercise test through being fat or stuffy, i.e. thick in the wind.

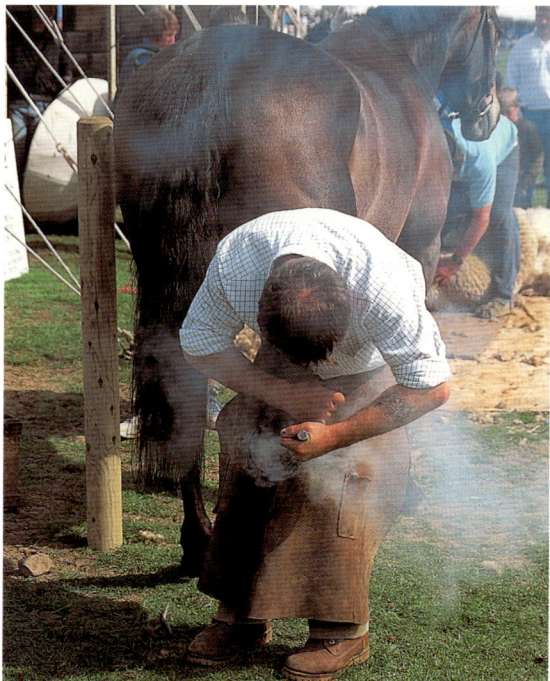

Apart from ensuring that the tack is adequate, the horse should be prepared for public scrutiny. It should not be truculent, resent being handled or be unruly. It should be capable of: being led at the walk and trot; cantering and galloping on a lunge or when ridden; and should not object to having its feet picked up, to being tested or to being handled generally.

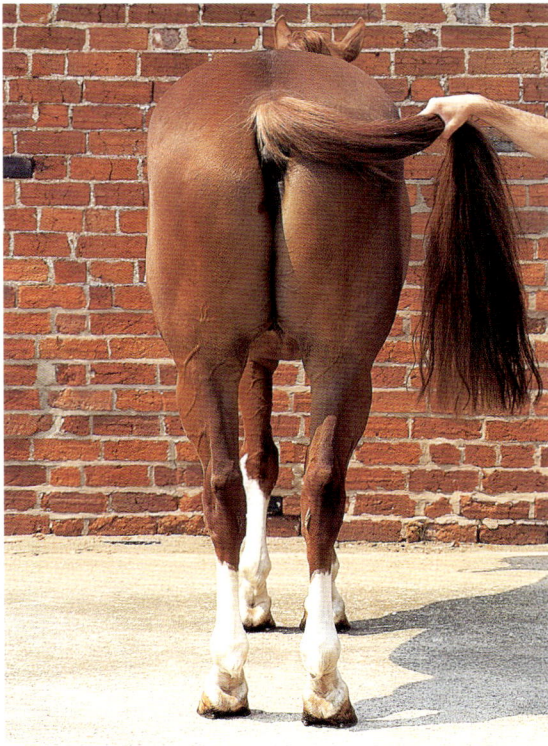

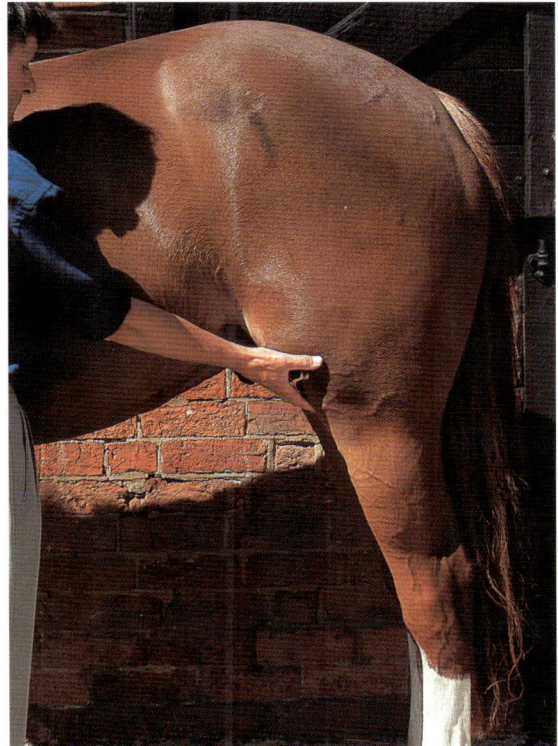

The condition of the feet is especially important, many sales fall through because a horse is presented with badly fitting shoes, or unprepared feet. The latter often happens because a vendor is saving money, expecting the buyer to have to pay for the farrier – an economy that has lost many a sale.

A horse that is ready and fit for examination is far more likely to pass than one which might refuse to go, or blow too easily and become distressed when tried, or make stuffy noises which could be mistaken for abnormal inspiratory noises linked with the larynx.

Should a horse be sold at a public sale, the vendor must know the conditions required for vetting. A sale may fall through if a horse is not presented within a given time spell; this could be as short as an hour from

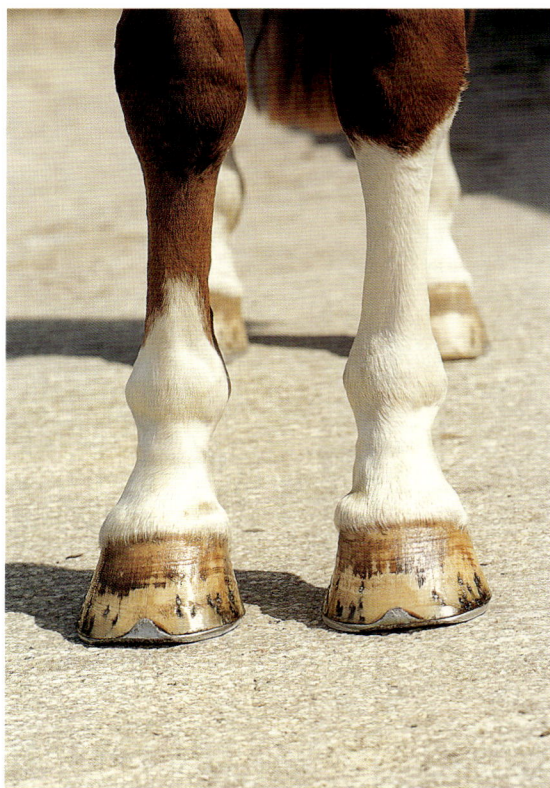

fall of hammer. It is important to ensure this requirement is expedited and the horse is available and properly attended throughout. A vetting will not take place unless the vendor, or an authorised agent, is present.

PRIVATE FACILITIES – STABLE, LUNGEING, RIDING

When a horse is being vetted privately, if this is being done at home or at a livery yard, it is essential that the animal is indoors for at least an hour before the vet arrives. It must be possible to darken the stable for examination of the eyes and it must be quiet for listening to the heart and lungs – although this part of the examination will also be pursued outside.

A vendor is not absolved of responsibility for an animal until all conditions of sale are complied with and the important details of payment and document transfer have been completed.

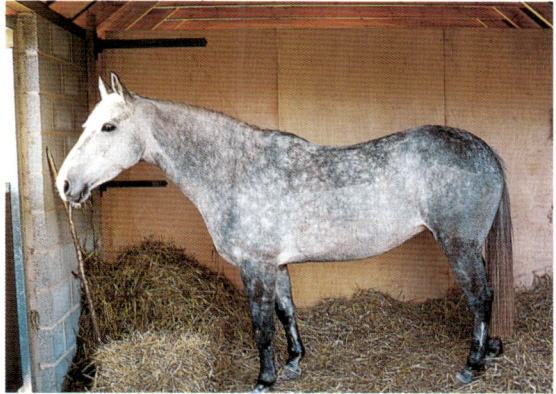

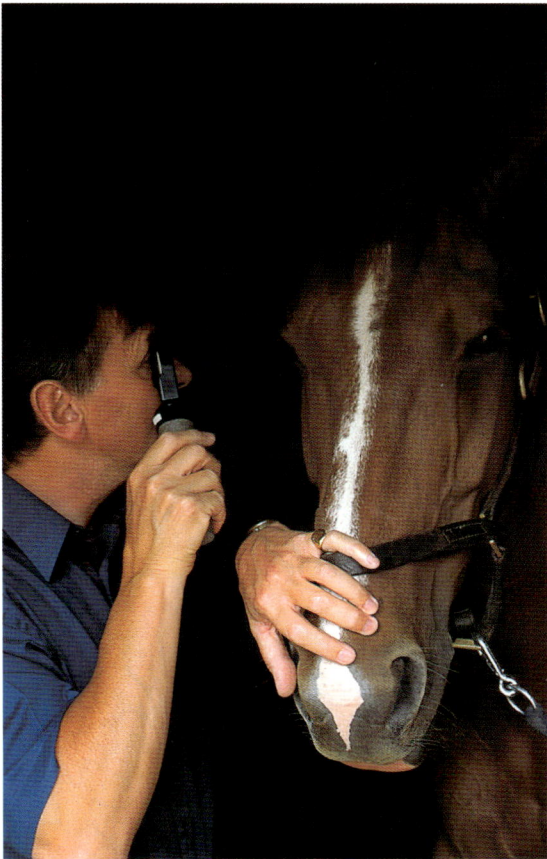

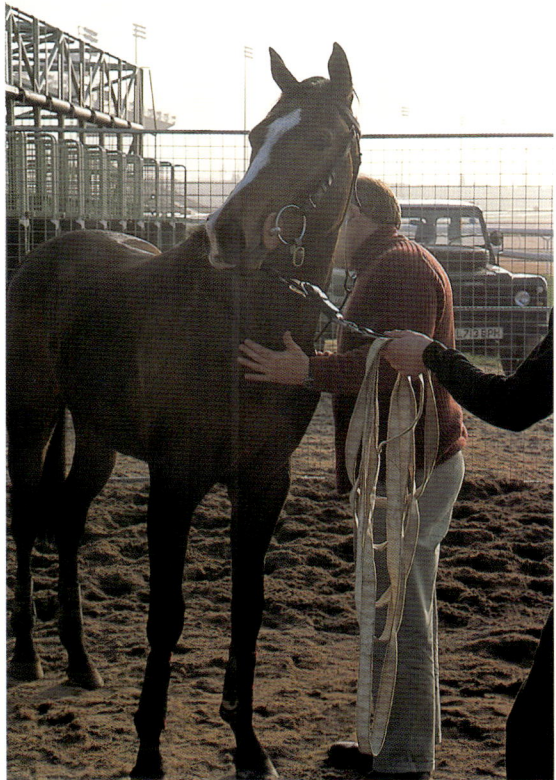

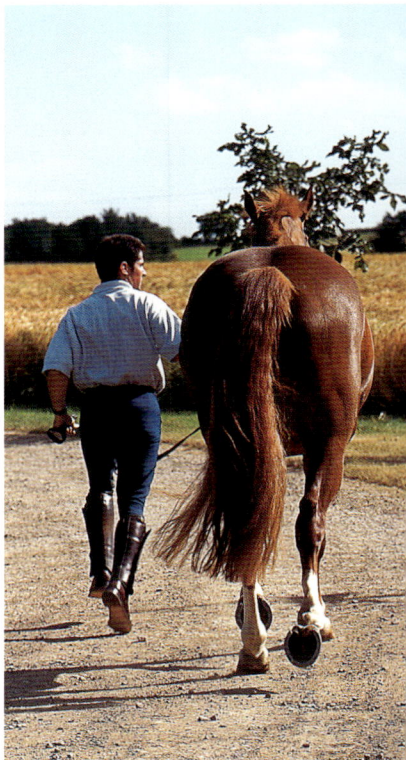

There must be a flat area of ground on which the horse can be inspected from all sides. There must also be a firm area where it can be walked and trotted back and forth for twenty or thirty metres. The animal must also be capable of being turned in either direction and reversed for a matter of metres.

Finally, there must be a suitable place for strenuous exercise to take place. A good lungeing area is needed, with an underfoot surface that is safe for both the horse and the handlers. If the horse is to be ridden, a large school, a field, or a gallop, will have to be available. Remember the degree of exercise the animal will be subjected to; the vet will want the horse to do adequate work to ensure it is blowing strongly, so that any abnormal inspiratory noises will be heard.

THE VET'S OPINION

The examination, for legal reasons mostly, is a contract between the buyer and the vet. The vet acts as the buyer's agent and addresses all opinions directly to that person. It is not a simple question of a horse being sound or unsound, of passing or failing. The vet is obliged to discuss all defects found and the sale is not completed until the buyer is satisfied. At any point, the sale may falter if the buyer is unhappy with the soundness of the animal. Naturally, this cannot be for frivolous reasons.

The vendor has no control over the veterinary opinion, and the sale falls through if the vet turns the animal down. It may be that further opinions are called in, or further tests demanded. However, this has to be by common consent and if a buyer does not want the horse on the basis of the first opinion, this would have to be respected, unless it could be established that the opinion was wrong, in which case other legal considerations might come into play for the vendor.

IMPORTANT POINTS

• The most common vetting procedure is pre-purchase examination.

• The vet acts for the buyer in this case.

• The vendor has no say in the outcome.

• If the vendor is not happy with the opinion, they should seek advice/a second opinion.

Finally, it is always advisable to be as accommodating as possible when selling, without going overboard. If radiographs are called for, or any other kind of test, they should be allowed. If blood is to be taken to test for the presence of masking drugs, they too should be agreed to. To object is only to create suspicion and the buyer could have blood taken immediately after a sale was completed. If the blood is taken with all due precautions, the result of the test might still hold sway if a dispute arose.

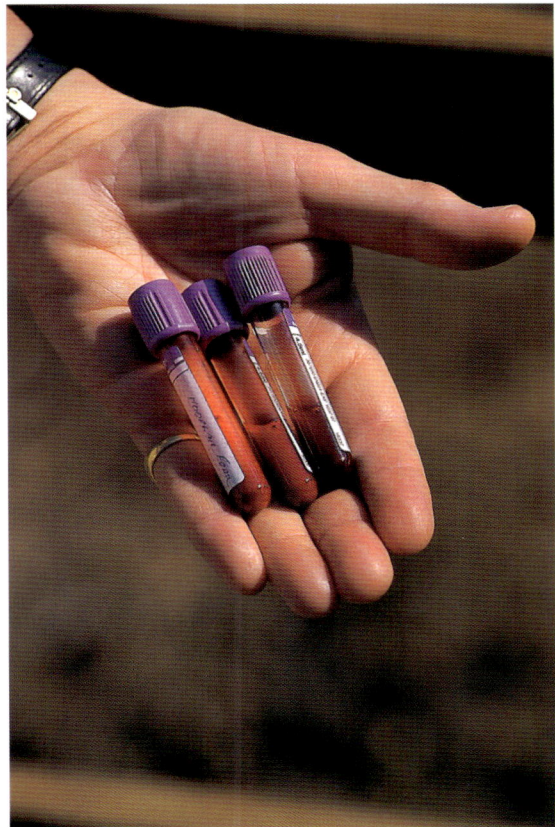

ACKNOWLEDGEMENTS

My thanks for the facilities and help go to: Sharon Baldwin of Meadow Stud; Brendan Paterson BVetMed, CertESM, MRCVS; Peter Jinman BVetMed, MRCVS; Mrs Wall of Bromyard; Michael and Averil Opperman of Tenbury Wells. Thanks also to all those others whose animals, or facilities, appear in this book.

British Library Cataloguing-in-Publication Data.
A catalogue record for this book is available from the British Library

ISBN 0.85131.750.2

© J. A. Allen 1999

Published in Great Britain in 1999 by
J. A. Allen an imprint of Robert Hale Ltd.,
Clerkenwell House, 45–47 Clerkenwell Green,
London EC1R 0HT

Design and Typesetting by Paul Saunders
Series editor Jane Lake
Colour processing by Tenon & Polert Colour Processing Ltd., Hong Kong
Printed in Hong Kong by Dah Hua International Printing Press Co. Ltd.